In Search of
Bede

by Simon Webb

Durham, 2010

First published by The Langley Press, 2010

ISBN: 978-0-9564551-2-3

The cover includes a view of the
Galilee chapel of Durham Cathedral from
R.W. Billings' *Architectural illustrations and description of the
Cathedral Church at Durham*, published in 1843.
Reprinted by kind permission of
Durham County Council

CONTENTS

The Fourth Heaven: Gustave Doré's illustration for Canto XII of Dante's Paradiso

I. A RIGHTEOUS SONG AND DANCE

In the third book of his poem *The Divine Comedy*, the Italian poet Dante Alighieri is given a guided tour of Heaven or, as he would have said in Italian, *Paradiso*.

Climbing higher and higher into Paradise, he enters the sun itself in Canto X. The sun contains the Fourth Heaven of Dante's universe. There he sees, dancing around himself and Beatrice his guide, a ring of twelve spirits, all holding hands and singing. These are saintly souls who were great scholars or teachers in life. They include Thomas Aquinas, Solomon, Boethius, Albertus Magnus, Peter the Lombard, and an Englishman who died in Northumbria in the eighth century - the Venerable Bede.

The fact that Bede is merely mentioned by name in the *Paradiso* and not described, may indicate that Dante's readers would immediately have known exactly who this remarkable man was in life, though he lived a long way from Italy, and nearly six hundred years before their time.

Dante also mentioned Bede in an angry letter to the cardinals of Florence, accusing them of allowing their copies of Bede's books to gather cobwebs in their cupboards, along with the works of St Ambrose and St Augustine[1].

Bede, who died in 735, may have been able to read books by or about five of his eleven dancing-companions during his life. These would have included Dionysius the Areopagite, who features in the New Testament Book of Acts, and the Spanish scholar Isidore of Seville, who died in 636. In fact the Northumbrian made regular use of Isidore's writings when he was writing his own books, and was even compiling a volume of extracts from Isidore at his death.

We know that Bede also used the writings of Paulus Orosius, another of his companions in the sun, when composing his own masterpiece, the *Ecclesiastical history of the English people*. Orosius, who was born in the fourth century, was a student of the African St Augustine, and dedicated his *History against the Pagans* to that saint.

Since Boethius died in the sixth century, we might expect that Bede would have read the works of that Roman philosopher, but it seems that Boethius was perhaps the most important writer known to the

---

1 *The Letters of Dante*, Ed. Paget Toynbee, Oxford, 1920, p.145 (Letter VIII)

Middle Ages, of whom Bede appears to have had no knowledge[2]. This may be due to the fact that Boethius didn't become popular until near the end of the eighth century.

It also seems doubtful that Bede had ever seen what he would have regarded as the works of Dionysius the Areopagite, which are now known to have been written centuries after the original Dionysius lived in Athens. Modern scholars attribute these works to 'the pseudo-Dionysius'. Bede had, however, *heard of* Dionysius, and he even mentions him on his own book *The Temple of Solomon*.

The Temple was Bede's attempt to prove that everything about Solomon's temple, as described in the Old Testament, symbolised or predicted something that was to happen in the later, Christian world. The temple itself symbolised the 'holy universal Church'; the famous cedars of Lebanon that were used in the construction stood for proud men who had been cast down and humiliated. Learned Christians like Dionysius were represented by the thousands of craftsmen who built the temple. Bede's *Temple of Solomon* provides us, therefore, with a triangular link between Bede and two of his heavenly dancing-partners: Dionysius the Areopagite and King Solomon.

There is also a firm link between Dionysius and Dante himself, who put Bede into the Fourth Heaven of his *Paradiso*: Dante is known to have used what he would have thought of as Dionysius' mystical works to construct the Heaven he describes in his great poem.

The six other men who dance with Bede in Heaven were born after the Northumbrian's death, so he could not have referred to their works when he was alive. If nothing else, Dante's *Divine Comedy* is a reminder that, after death, one may meet the souls of people one could never have met, read or even heard about in life.

If he had been able to understand Dante's convoluted fourteenth-century poetic Italian, Bede would probably have enjoyed the canto in which he features. Before it gets to the dancing worthies, this part of the *Paradiso* mentions the movements of the sun and the stars, and describes how the sun behaves at Easter; a Christian festival which was an interest, if not an obsession, of Bede's.

Another connection between Bede and Dante is that they were both very keen on the works of the Roman poet Virgil, who was born in 70

2　See Laistner, M.L.W.: *The library of the Venerable Bede*, in *Bede: His life, times and writings*, ed. Thompson, p. 262

6

BC. Bede was able to quote suitable Latin tags from Virgil in some of his works; and one of the major sources for Dante's *Divine Comedy* is Virgil's narrative poem the *Aeneid*. Virgil himself features in Dante's epic as the poet's guide to Hell and Purgatory.

An interesting example of how the written word is able to link Bede, Virgil and Dante across the centuries is to be found in the shape of the mythical three-headed dog, Cerberus. This original 'Hound of Hell' appears in Hades in Virgil's *Aeneid,* where he acts as guard-dog to the Land of the Dead. He also turns up in Dante's *Inferno*, where he is employed in eternally tormenting the souls of those who were guilty in life of the sin of gluttony. In Bede's *Letter to Egbert*[3], Cerberus is used as a symbol for the more general sin of greed, which Bede tells us includes the 'plagues' of drunkenness, gluttony and extravagance.

There is a chance that Bede had the sixth book of the *Aeneid* in the back of his mind as he wrote the *Letter to Egbert*, as both are preoccupied with justice, and criticise those who distort or misuse the law for their own wicked purposes.

In Canto XII of the *Paradiso* Dante sees another circle of twelve more spirits, who must be more spaced out, as they dance round Bede and his companions, forming a larger ring. This second holy dozen contains, among others, St Bonaventure, St Anselm, and Nathan, the Old Testament prophet. From this outer circle, Bede is known to have used the works of St John Chrysostom, and Donatus, a fourth-century Bishop of Carthage. Later a third circle appears, but Dante is unable to identify anyone in it before he is whisked off to Mars.

Strange as it may seem, the Northumbria of Bede's day had its own equivalent of Dante – its own astronaut of the afterlife. This was one Dryhthelm, who died, came back to life, and proceeded to tell certain people what he had seen of the life after death, through which he was guided by 'a man of shining countenance and wearing bright robes'. There he saw a version of Purgatory where the dead souls were compelled to jump repeatedly out of a freezing-cold place into a fire, and then back into the cold. He also saw Hell in the form of a stinking, burning pit, and the very edge of Heaven – a walled garden with sweetly-scented flowers.

Bede recorded Dryhthelm's journey in detail in his *Ecclesiastical history*, which suggests not only that he believed the man, but that he

---

3   In the Oxford *Ecclesiastical history*, translated by McClure and Collins.

also thought his story needed to be passed on. Deeply affected by his vision, Dryhthelm later became a monk at Melrose and mortified his flesh with punishments, such as praying while standing up to his neck in a freezing river.

We might think Bede was naïve to believe such a tale, but that would be to forget that Bede lived during the age of saints and miracles in the Northumbrian church. An interesting aspect of the story is that Hell and Heaven have their own distinctive smells – the latter of which is of course delightful. This suggests that the spiritual realm takes care to appeal to all the senses when it intrudes into mundane life.

In pictures, Bede is not usually depicted, as Dante shows him, dancing, but rather sitting, kneeling or lying down and either reading, writing, praying or dictating. Considering the strict monastic life he lived, and the immense amount of scholarly writing he achieved, it seems doubtful that Bede would ever have had the time or opportunity to dance. In Paradise, however, no more reading or writing is necessary. There the scholars can spend eternity celebrating the God who created the universe they tried to make some sense of in life.

Though he may not have had much experience of dancing, Bede would have spent many hours of his life singing: the singing or chanting of psalms in the 'antiphonal' style was a crucial part of monastic life in the west of Europe in the seventh and eighth centuries. In fact the monks were so accustomed to singing that they could break into song spontaneously and, like a modern soccer crowd, fit their song to the prevailing mood[4]. When the abbey at Jarrow was almost wiped out by plague, Ceolfrith the abbot couldn't bear to stop the singing, and he ended up singing together with only one other person – a small boy who some think may have been Bede himself[5].

We now call the style of singing used by the monks at this time plainsong, or Gregorian chant after Pope Gregory I (d. 604), who codified the church music of his times. According to Bede's disciple Cuthbert (who is not to be confused with Saint Cuthbert) the Northumbrian saint continued singing praises to God almost until the last hour of his life.

The community in which Bede lived had been taught the correct

---

4 See *The anonymous history of Abbot Ceolfrith* in Webb, J.F., *The age of Bede,* p. 222
5 Ibid, p. 218

way to sing the psalms by no less a person than the chief cantor of St Peter's in Rome - a man called Abbot John of Tours. He had travelled to Northumbria with Benedict Biscop, the founder of the monasteries at Wearmouth and Jarrow. John, who had been sent to the northern fastness by the pope himself, had probably become part of the monastery of Wearmouth around the time Bede joined it, as a boy of seven. He found time to record his musical ideas in books, which were designed to transmit them to readers after his death.

John was also present at an important synod at Hatfield at about this time. He had also brought a sort of certificate of approval of the monastery of Wearmouth from Pope Agatho, and had been commanded by the pope to inquire into the Christianity of the Northumbrians, to sniff out any leanings toward heresy.

II. A MONK'S LIFE

Bede was probably born in either 672 or 673. Over a hundred years after his birth, a king called Biscop was succeeded by someone called Bede in the kingdom of Lindsey, which was roughly equivalent to modern Lincolnshire. (In Bede's day Britain was divided into many kingdoms, some smaller than the average modern county). Because names pass down through families, the information about this king called Bede has suggested to some scholars that the earlier Bede, the Northumbrian monk, was related in some way to the royal family of Lindsey. If that was the case, then we must also consider the possibility that Benedict Biscop, the founder of the monastery in which Bede lived, came from the same background.

The theory about the Lindsey kings and their relationship to Bede and Biscop seems more credible when we consider that the names of both of these men are unusual. Names usually have meanings, and the name 'Bede' may be related to the Anglo-Saxon word 'bēd', meaning prayer, though we shouldn't forget that Bede's real name was probably something like 'Bæda' or 'Beda'. 'Biscop' means 'bishop', which tends to suggest that Biscop's parents were Christians with pious ambitions for their son. It was only later that Biscop acquired the additional name 'Benedict', perhaps because he used the Rule of St

Benedict in constructing a Rule for his own monastery[6]. All this happened long before English people started to acquire surnames.

If Bede and Biscop were both the children of pious aristocrats from Lindsey, then Bede's admission to the monastery at Wearmouth at the age of seven begins to look like the story of an aristocratic boy who was left in the care of something like his uncle or great-uncle (Biscop was some forty-four years older than Bede).

The fact that Bede tells us, in his *Ecclesiastical history*, that he was born and raised on the lands of the monastery he later joined does not militate against the theory of a family relationship between Bede and Biscop. It may be that Bede was raised in some settlement on the monastery lands (while Biscop kept an eye on him from a distance) until he seemed to be of an age to enter the monastery. True, Bede does not tell us that he was Biscop's nephew, but then he and Biscop were both very much against nepotism in monasteries. Although the rulers of the little kingdoms that then dominated Britain were usually succeeded by their sons, nephews or brothers, the monks were supposed to elect their abbots. This was stipulated in the Rule of St Benedict, and certificates such as the one Abbot John had brought from Rome were supposed to guarantee the monks' democratic rights in this respect.

It is impossible to say whether Bede benefited from nepotism in the progress of his career. He was made a deacon at the age of nineteen, six years earlier than canon law dictated, but then after being made a priest at the age of thirty, he seems to have gone no further up the religious hierarchy. That Bede was made a deacon so young may of course be because the monasteries at Wearmouth and Jarrow were still short of monks as a result of the plague that struck when Bede was about twelve years old.

That Bede was allowed to consume expensive resources like parchment in the writing of his books may suggest a certain privilege, but then the obvious merit of these works, and their usefulness to their intended readers, probably pleaded in favour of their being allowed to be written, despite the expense.

If there really was no nepotism involved in the relationship between Bede and Biscop, then Bede may really have been a local boy, the son

---

6   There is a discussion of the Rule of St Benedict in relation to the lost Rule of Benedict Biscop in the first chapter of Wormald, *The times of Bede*, Blackwell, 2006.

of ordinary but pious parents, who entered a monastery and rose to become one of the most important men of the early middle ages.

It was not uncommon for parents, particularly aristocratic ones, to 'donate' a child or two to monasteries or nunneries. This may seem heartless, but people did tend to have more children then, and pious Christian parents no doubt thought that the monastic life was a good life in the spiritual sense.

Given the diseases and wars that were so prevalent in Anglo-Saxon times, as well as the risks associated with child-birth, it is quite possible that Bede was an orphan, who was put in the monastery by his surviving relatives because they couldn't care for him. Bede doesn't mention his parents in the little autobiography he writes into his *History*, an omission that would be understandable if he'd never known them, or couldn't remember them.

Procedures for receiving boys given to a monastery are set down in the Rule of St Benedict, which seems to have been the foundation of the Rule adhered to by the monks of Wearmouth/Jarrow. The donors had to draw up a special document, and had to promise that, by entering the monastery, the boy was giving up any expectations of inheriting wealth or power later in life. Benedict's words in this part of his Rule suggest that the expectation of future wealth had ruined the spiritual progress of some of his monks. Benedict was, however, happy to receive no-strings donations of money or property to the monastery from the parents of donated boys.

If the words of Benedict's Rule were followed to the letter at Wearmouth, Bede would have undergone a solemn ceremony on first being officially received into the monastery, during which his hands would have been bound in an altar-cloth, together with the special document drawn up by his guardians. The life Bede escaped by entering the monastery at an early age was indeed a harsh life, even for the aristocrats who lived at the top of the hierarchy. Archaeology has revealed that few Anglo-Saxons lived beyond the age of forty, and that they were the victims of all sorts of nasty diseases, including plague, leprosy and tuberculosis, which the primitive medicine of the time could do little about.

The lifestyle of the typical Anglo-Saxon would seem very uncomfortable to any time-travellers from our century foolish enough to get stranded in theirs. Unlike the Romans who came before them, the Anglo-Saxons tended to build not in stone but in wood, often making the walls of their buildings out of wattle panels daubed with a kind of primitive plaster, which included animal dung as one of its constituents. The resulting buildings ranged from huts and hovels to magnificent halls where kings and thanes[7] would feast their followers, consuming vast quantities of mead and stuffing themselves with pork in season.

At times, though, these Anglo-Saxon buildings must have offered little protection from the unusually bitter winters of the period. They were also horribly subject to fire. Because of the ever-present risk of war, settlements were usually surrounded by a ditch, and some sort of fence to keep out invaders, as well as marauding wolves and bears.

The Anglo-Saxons did not lack high culture, and the poem *Beowulf* shows that they were capable of the most complex types of art. Despite its veneer of Christianity *Beowulf* is, however, clearly the product of a barbaric culture, obsessed with violence.

Many Anglo-Saxon men and even small children were buried with weapons, including spears which, it seems, all free men carried about with them all the time. Some of the most magnificent archaeological finds from the period are associated with war – these include helmets (some with terrifying masks to cover the face), shield-bosses and swords.

The hundreds of Saxon items found in a field in Staffordshire in 2009 may all have a warlike connection, even though some of them are apparently peaceful objects such as gold crosses and finger-rings. It is thought that this amazing hoard may consist entirely of items stripped from the bodies of dead warriors after a battle, or of objects taken from prisoners of war, who in those days might have been sold into slavery after their goods had been confiscated.

The idea that the Staffordshire Saxon hoard might consist of the spoils of war is reinforced by the fact that some gold items show signs of having been quite literally stripped off other artefacts made of less valuable materials. Gold sword-hilts and pommels, and the curious little 'sword pyramids' had been parted from sword-blades, while gold shield-ornaments were found to have been twisted in the process of being prised off. The crosses found in the Staffordshire hoard may have been intended for use as standards in battle.

---

7   Or 'thegns', military followers of the king, also aristocrats (from Old English).

Some Anglo-Saxon burials show signs that the people buried died of injuries suffered in combat. The landed gentry of Anglo-Saxon times were required to wage war pretty regularly to defend the land they claimed as theirs, and we can picture figures like the aristocratic Benedict Biscop putting aside their swords, helmets and shields and replacing them with goose-quill pens, tonsures and woollen hoods.

During Bede's lifetime King Ceolwulf of the Kingdom of Northumbria became a monk twice, though his first donning of the monk's hood was not voluntary. At some point he was deposed by person or persons unknown, and forced to become a monk at the island monastery of Lindisfarne, a place forever associated with the names of St Cuthbert, St Oswald and St Aidan. Somehow Ceolwulf was able to regain his kingdom in 730, but he abdicated to become a Lindisfarne monk again in 737. It is said that, because they were now living with a king, the monks were allowed to drink wine and beer instead of just water and milk.

The contrast Ceolwulf experienced between life as a warrior-king and life as a monk must have been considerable, but warriors and monks shared parts of a common ethos: as far as they were concerned, the monks were valiant soldiers for Christ, who used inner weapons to fight their great adversary, the devil.

Ceolwulf is important to the story of Bede because it was to this king that he dedicated his *Ecclesiastical history.* Although his dedication, and the words of Bede's *Letter to Egbert,* give the impression that Ceolwulf was learned and pious, later in his *History* Bede acknowledges that his reign was 'filled with so many and such serious commotions and setbacks that it is as yet impossible to know what to say about them or to guess what the outcome will be'. These 'commotions and setbacks' were happening despite the fact that, as Bede tells us near the end of his *Ecclesiastical history,* England was enjoying a period of comparative peace around the year 731.

It may be that Ceolwulf's concern for the church went against the grain of the Northumbrian aristocracy through which he was supposed to rule. Warfare between and within the petty kingdoms of Anglo-Saxon England was part of the prevalent culture, and a king with a spiritual side might have had to be extra-warlike at times so as not to appear weak. It may be that Ceolwulf resembled Shakespeare's King Henry VI: a pious man whose saintly concerns distracted him from the business of state-craft.

In any case, Ceolwulf was not unique in giving up his throne to pursue the religious life. Cædwalla, the ruthless king of the West Saxons, abdicated and went on a pilgrimage to Rome, where he was baptised in 689 and died while still in his white baptismal robes. Cenred the king of Mercia also abdicated and went to Rome, where he became a monk. Æthelred, his predecessor, later became an abbot at Bardney, in what is now Lincolnshire.

Ceolwulf was made a saint after his death, and his head ended up as one of the treasured relics of Durham Cathedral. He was depicted 'upon the screen work of the altar of Saint Jerome and Saint Benedict'[8] in the cathedral, along with other famous Christians, including St Gregory, St Oswald and Pope Hadrian IV, the only English pope so far, who ruled in the middle of the twelfth century[9].

Although Bede's monastery had papal guarantees of independence, it still relied on the local bishop and the local monarch for support, advice and protection. It was on land granted by Ecgfrith, the king of Northumbria, to Benedict Biscop, that the monastery of Wearmouth was founded it 674.

Biscop, who is one of the heroes of Bede's *Lives of the Abbots of Wearmouth and Jarrow,* was by no means the type of abbot to remain forever in his monastery and take a hands-on approach to the detail of everyday monastic life. He was an inveterate traveller who made five or six trips to Rome – no mean feat in those days of poor (or non-existent) roads and small, fragile wooden boats.

As we have already seen, he brought the musical Abbot John from Rome to Britain, and he also brought glaziers and stone-masons from France to put up his monastery buildings. He was responsible for bringing many very valuable artefacts back from the Continent to embellish his foundation, including church plate, vestments, pictures and (what was most important for Bede's future) many books, and a number of calendars.

Even before 664, when the Synod of Whitby determined that the English Church would adopt the Roman Catholic ways, Rome had been a favourite destination for international pilgrimages from the British Isles. The Eternal City was not only the home of the pope – it

---

8 See *The Rites of Durham*, published by the Surtees Society, pp.124-143
9 See my *Nicholas Breakspear, the pope from England* (2009)

14

was also the resting-place of the apostles Peter and Paul.

One possible consequence of Continental trips such as those made by Biscop was that infectious diseases, including plague, could be brought into the English monasteries. Plague is mentioned very regularly in the writings of Bede and his contemporaries, and although we usually associate the bubonic plague in Europe with the fourteenth century and later, there is pretty strong evidence that this type of pestilence could have been in England in the seventh and eighth centuries.

It may be that the plagues that wiped out so many of Bede's monkish brothers were later waves of the disease that struck Constantinople in the middle of the sixth century, and even infected the Emperor Justinian himself. By definition, bubonic plague is associated with swelling, and in both Bede's *Life of St Cuthbert* and a life of Cuthbert by an anonymous monk of Lindisfarne, there is mention of the bodies of plague victims swelling up[10].

We now know that bubonic plague, which last visited England in the seventeenth century, was typically spread by fleas living on rats. Many of Bede's more pious contemporaries thought it virtuous to wash very seldom, and the fleas of Wearmouth and Jarrow must have had a pretty easy time of it. The monastery was, on one level, a large farm, and even today farms have rats – Bede's monastery would also have had a wide range of domesticated animals on which the fleas could have thrived. Bubonic plague tends to be more virulent in hot weather – the most likely time of year for Biscop, his attendant monks and perhaps his horses to travel to and from the Continent.

In a book on the plagues of this period[11], William Rosen speculates that places like Wearmouth and Jarrow could have been more likely to attract plague as they were both on rivers and near the sea. The plague bacterium, *Yersinia pestis*, was carried by ship-rats that were particularly attracted to ships transporting grain.

If the visitation followed its normal course, the animals in the settlement would have developed bubonic plague about two weeks before the humans – when the monks started to be affected, as many as seventy percent of them would have died in less than a fortnight. Apart from the characteristic swelling (caused by the bacterium's

---

10 See Colgrave's *Two lives of St Cuthbert*, pp. 119 and 181
11 Rosen, William: *Justinian's flea*, 2006

attack on the lymph system), symptoms would have included vomiting, abdominal pain, diarrhoea, headache, chills, fever and the appearance of tiny broken blood vessels, called *petechiae*, just under the surface of the skin.

The monks and secular clergy of Bede's time sometimes demonstrated scant regard for the possibility that they might be spreading infection on their travels – the crucial synod of Whitby happened in 664 – a particularly bad plague year.

As well as books, pictures, devotional items and, perhaps, disease, Biscop must have brought with him from the Continent some idea of how a monastery should look. We must not, however, imagine Biscop's first monastery at Wearmouth to have been an immense stone complex with soaring gothic arches and vast vaulted cellars, such as we can discern in the ruins of, say, Fountains Abbey in North Yorkshire. Wearmouth was, however, rather grander than the huddles of wooden buildings that comprised many monasteries in the British Isles at the time.

Archaeology at Wearmouth and at its sister monastery at Jarrow has revealed the remains of stone buildings with glass windows and roofs of stone slates supported by timbers. One of the buildings at Jarrow may even have had two storeys. There were floors made of *opus signinum* – a mixture of broken tiles and concrete[12] – and smooth walls coated with mortar.

The presence of glass – both coloured and plain – in these buildings was an historic first for England: imported glass was used at York before this, but it was not actually made there. At Jarrow, archaeologists have found evidence of a glass-making workshop.

The masons at these sites 'cheated' in that they got a lot of their stone from old Roman buildings – a reminder that Benedict, Bede and their contemporaries were still living among the remains of the great civilisation that had collapsed in the west, and had deserted Britain nearly three hundred years before Bede was born.

If he really lived on the lands of the monastery until he himself entered it, Bede would have seen the buildings at Wearmouth being put up. He may even have watched, fascinated, as the alien craftsmen with their strange speech melted and coloured glass, dressed stones,

---

12 Concrete seems like a very modern building material but it was used in ancient times – parts of the Colosseum in Rome were made of concrete.

made concrete and skimmed the walls with creamy mortar.

Bede would have seen the whole process repeated when Jarrow began to go up, shortly after he entered the monastery at Wearmouth. Jarrow was built on an extra grant of land from the Northumbrian King Ecgfrith to Biscop, and there is some debate as to whether Bede spent most of his life there, or at the slightly older sister monastery of Wearmouth.

The idea that Bede moved to Jarrow as soon as that monastery was habitable is partly based on the aforementioned story in the *Anonymous life of Ceolfrith*[13] which states that, when the plague visited Jarrow in 685/6, only Abbot Ceolfrith and a small boy were left to sing the psalms in church. For a long time, it was accepted that the small boy in question was Bede himself, but in the introduction to their edition of the *Ecclesiastical history* McClure and Collins argue that the Latin word used for this little boy, *puerulus*, would not have been applied to a boy of twelve or thirteen, which is how old Bede would have been when the plague struck Jarrow.

Another piece of evidence in favour of Bede having spent most of his time at Jarrow is that his bones were stolen from the church there during the eleventh century. McClure and Collins remind us that the truth about where Bede was buried may have become lost during the three centuries and more between Bede's death and the theft of his bones, but Simeon of Durham, writing perhaps fifty years after the theft, seems pretty certain that the theft was from Jarrow.[14]

Given the extent of Bede's reading and writing in later life, it is likely that he spent his time wherever the monastery library was, but we don't know if that was concentrated at Wearmouth or at Jarrow. Given the high value of the books, the ever-present risk of fire and the fact that there must have been more than one copy of some volumes, it is likely that the collection Biscop and others assembled was dispersed between the two houses. In that case we can picture Bede, in his years of health, walking between the two libraries and, when he became too old or busy to do this, sending other monks off to fetch books he needed, and to return others he'd finished with.

Wherever he spent most of his time, Bede insists in his own writings that the two monasteries were to be counted as one monastery in two

---

13 In Webb, J.F. (ed.): *The Age of Bede*
14 Simeon of Durham: *A history of the church of Durham*, p. 679

different places, governed by the same Rule and with a high degree of cooperation between all the monks of both houses.

As Bede grew up among the monks, he would have learned Latin, Greek and perhaps Hebrew; the correct manner of singing the psalms in church, and how to write on the parchment (also called vellum), made from animal skins, that the monks used as paper. His whole life would not, however, have been entirely devoted to these scholarly pursuits.

In his *Lives of the abbots* Bede describes how Eosterwine, abbot of Wearmouth, enjoyed all the daily tasks of the monastery, although he himself had been born into a noble family, and was a cousin to Benedict Biscop. Eosterwine would winnow and thresh the corn, milk the sheep and cows, follow the plough, tend the garden and work in the kitchen, bakery and forge. All this was in keeping with the Rule of St Benedict, which has a lot to say about the importance of manual work, and the need for monasteries to be self-contained and to live off their own resources.

Benedict's Rule, which may have formed the basis for the Rule at Wearmouth/Jarrow, was less harsh than that followed by some of the Egyptian originators of Christian monasticism. Benedict did not approve of the asceticism, or deliberate hard-living, that groups like the Celtic Christian monks indulged in. He suggested, for instance, that a pint of wine per day was quite adequate for the needs of a monk, and that he should have a mattress and a pillow to sleep on, and two blankets to keep him warm at night. Benedict also suggests that each monk should have two sets of clothes, to allow for one set to be washed.

Benedict's Rule emphasises the importance of humility as part of a monk's character, and places the Abbot very much at the centre of monastic life. His word was law, and, particularly as it applied to young boys, his law could be tough. Benedict recommended harsh beatings and starvation for badly-behaved boys, adolescents and men, under certain circumstances.

Bede sharpening his pen, © Miranda Brown, from a picture at Engelberg Monastery, Switzerland

Virgil meets Cerberus in Dante's Inferno - Gustave Doré

The Galilee Chapel by Billings (Durham County Council)

PRIMOS	HΓOYMENOYC
INFRATRIBUS	ENTOICAΔEΛϕοιc
SCRIBENTES	ΓΡΑΨΑΝΤΕC
PERMANUM	ΔIAXEIPOC
EORUM	ΛΥTωN
hAEC	TAΛE
APOSTOLI	OIAΠOCΓOΛOI
ETSENIORES	KAIOIΠΡΕCБYτερoι
ETFRATRES	KAIOIΛΛEΛϕoι
hISquISUNTANTIUChIAE	TOICKATATHHANTιoXιᾱ
ETSUNAE·ETCILICIAE:	KAICYPIAH·KAICιΛιΚιᾱ
FRATRIBUS	ΛΛEΛϕOIC
quISUNTEXGENTIBUS	TOICEZEΘNωN
SALUTEM	XAIPEIN
quONIAM	EΠIΔH
AudiuIMUS	HKOYCAMEN
quIA	OTI
quIDAM	TINEC
EXNObIS	EZHMωN
EXEUNTES	EZEΛΘONTEC
TURBAUERUNT	ETAΡΑΝ
UOS	ΥMAC
UERbIS	ΛOΓOIC
EUERTENTES	ANΛCICEYΛZONτec

Page from the Codex Laudianus, showing columns of Latin and Greek (Wikimedia Commons)

Ezra, from the Codex Amiatinus (© Miranda Brown)

Monkwearmouth Church in 1819 (Durham County Council)

Jarrow Church in the 1840s (Durham County Council)

St Cuthbert (right), one of Bede's heroes, from Raine's St Cuthbert (Durham County Council)

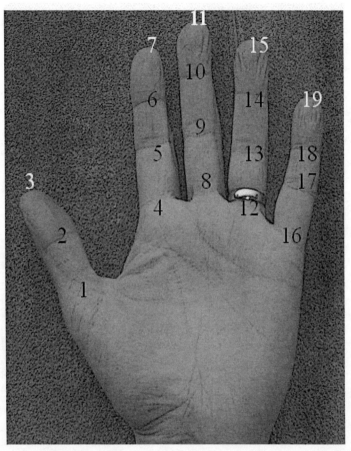

Bede's method of counting to 19 on the fingers of one hand (photo © Patricia Brown)

III. BEDE THE TEACHER

No doubt Bede was also expected to help with the farming and cooking, and labour in the workshops, but as his scholarly propensities began to emerge, he may have been encouraged to spend more and more time reading, writing and teaching.

Bede was above all a teacher: whether he was teaching his brother monks directly, or through his books, his concern seems to have been to absorb knowledge and understanding from the past and then re-present it in a clear and accurate way, thus aiding its transmission into the future.

Some of the texts attributed to Bede show signs of having been intended as an early form of text-book or reference-book. In the *Ecclesiastical history* there are useful chapter-headings, and summaries of the historic events described – these summaries were inserted by Bede, as he tells us, to assist memory.

As teacher and writer, Bede showed very little willingness to specialise – he would never be the equivalent of a teacher who only taught Latin grammar, for instance. His interests and knowledge ranged over a huge area, from languages and literature to poetry and song, the study of the Bible, history (of course) and science.

Bede was able to connect the very diverse subjects he was interested in in all sorts of ways. Since his ultimate aim was to promote and deepen the Christian faith, which was relatively new to the Anglo-Saxons, Bede was enthusiastic about adapting scientific knowledge, including knowledge from the ancient Pagan world, to his Christian purposes.

A remarkable and elaborate example of Bede's use of science to aid religion is his work on time. The scholar was not only interested in how thinking about time could help his historical studies – he also wanted to use his knowledge of time to solve what was a thorny problem for Christians loyal to Rome – the date of Easter.

In the twenty-first century, everybody knows well in advance when Easter Sunday will fall because we all have access to calendars and diaries, either in paper or electronic form. In Bede's time this was not the case, and for centuries scholars struggled to devise a calendar that would enable the user to to know the exact day when Easter Sunday was to be celebrated.

Unlike Christmas Day, Easter Sunday can fall on a different date every year – in fact in the modern western system Easter Sunday can fall on any date between March 22nd and April 25th. This is because Easter commemorates the resurrection of Christ, which the Gospels tell us happened at the time of the Jewish festival of Passover. Passover is supposed to happen on the first full moon after the spring equinox. This was easy for the Jews to calculate, because they used a lunar calendar. It was harder for the Christians, because they were using the old Roman solar calendar, and always wanted to celebrate Easter on a Sunday. The problem was, how to mesh these two types of calendars together so that the Christians would always know when Easter fell.

The Christians could not use the same calendar every year – this would be like using, say, the calendar you started using on the first of January last year, for this year. If you attempted this, you would immediately find yourself out of step with everyone else – you might even lose track of what day of the week it was.

Bede's solution to this problem was to promote the use of a giant nineteen-year calendar which, in theory, would fit in with the phases of the moon and the seasons of the year forever, if the nineteen-year cycle was started on the right day and repeated accurately every nineteen years. The idea was not original to Bede, but he had worked out for himself that this was the best system of its type.

Going back to the image of Bede and his eleven partners dancing in the sun, we might try to visualise this system of nineteen years as nineteen dancers dancing through the centuries. Dante tells us that the rings of dancers in the sun would pause occasionally, as if to listen for a new rhythm. In the nineteen-year cycle, the equivalents of these pauses were the various days and groups of days that had to be added to, and subtracted from, certain years within the cycle to keep it synchronised with the movements of the sun and moon.

Other people attempted this using cycles of different numbers of years – an eighty-four year cycle was very popular, but the nineteen-year system was nearer to what was needed. One advantage of the Northumbrian's preferred system was that the number nineteen could be counted out on the fingers of one hand.

In our modern world of pocket-calculators and cheap pencils with which to scribble sums, nobody needs to count higher than five on each hand, but it is possible to count to nineteen on one hand by counting the fourteen joints of the hand, and adding the tops of the four fingers and the top of the thumb. Bede believed that because this number was the same as the number of years in his beloved nineteen-year cycle, people would find it easier to use the nineteen-year system. Bede also described a system of counting to twenty-eight, and even to nine thousand nine hundred and ninety-nine, using just the fingers of both hands.

Bede set out his ideas on time in his book *The reckoning of time*, which was the second of his two books on the subject. This book also shows signs that it was intended as a teaching text – the finger-counting system is itself an aid to memory; and in his introductory chapters Bede presents alternative starting-points for readers setting out with different levels of preliminary knowledge.

In *The reckoning of time*, Bede also attempts a brief history and chronology of the world, beginning with the Creation. In this world-chronicle Bede counts the years using not the BC/AD system which he popularised, but the older system of counting from the year of Creation.

Bede's world-chronicle combines his biblical and historical knowledge with his fascination for time. By counting the years and generations given in the Bible and other sources, he arrives at the conclusion that, in his time, the world was less that five thousand years old. By counting the years from Creation, he puts the birth of Christ in the year 3952. By this system, Bede was born around 4624, and the year 2000 was the year 5952.

When Bede included the first version of his world chronicle in *On times*, his first book about time, he got into serious trouble. The problem was that by calculating that Jesus had been born in the year 3952, he had seemingly contradicted the old idea that Jesus had been born during the Sixth Age of the world. At what Bede describes as a drunken dinner at Hexham, where he himself was not present, somebody accused Bede of heresy in this matter, in the hearing of the powerful Wilfrid, Bishop of Northumbria.

Bede's contemporaries believed that history could be divided into six ages, because Genesis told them that the world had been created in six days. The fourth-century Christian historian Eusebius had calculated that Jesus was born in 5199, which put his birth inside the sixth millennium since Creation. Bede's critics supposed that all six ages of world history had been a thousand years long, so they made a malicious case for Bede having moved the Nativity back to the Fourth Age of the world.

Bede answered the charge of heresy in his *Letter to Plegwin*, where he explained that he believed Jesus had been born in the Sixth Age, but that the Six Ages could not possibly have all been one thousand years long. The First Age, from Adam to Noah, had been 1656 years while the Second, from Noah to Abraham, had been just 292 years.

Its seems that Plegwin, the addressee of this letter, was supposed to give it to someone called David, who was then supposed to read it aloud to Bishop Wilfrid. Whether or not the letter reached the ears of the bishop, and whether or not he understood it and agreed with it, it seems that the charge of heresy against Bede was not pursued.

Although he was at heart a teacher, Bede had no illusions about the level of ability among his students. In the preface to a book explaining the Book of Revelation, he explained that, because the people of his race were lazy, forgetful and reluctant to read, he was forced to be as brief as possible in his explanations and in his sentences.

IV. A WORLD OF BOOKS

It is clear that, in order to write books such as *The reckoning of time*, Bede had to have access to a sizeable library. Books were particularly important to medieval scholars such as Bede because originality was not well-regarded in his time, and ideas were better respected if they could be backed up with references to acknowledged authorities. In the *Letter to Plegwin* alone, Bede refers to Bibles in the Hebrew, Greek and Latin languages, to the works of Isidore of Seville, to Origen, Jerome, Josephus, Augustine of Hippo, and Eusebius.

The catalogue of Bede's library has been lost, but by surveying Bede's surviving works it has been possible for modern scholars to make a guess at the books Bede could lay his hands on. In a list appended to his article on *The library of the Venerable Bede*,[15] Laistner lists over eighty authors Bede must have read. For St

---

15 In Thompson (ed.): *Bede, His life, times and writings*, p.237 ff.

Augustine alone, Laistner finds evidence for Bede's use of nearly twenty works. The list of authors includes the aforementioned Eusebius, Orosius, Josephus, Virgil and Isidore of Seville, along with the heretic Pelagius, Pliny, and the British historian Gildas. Combining the works of all these authors that Bede seems to have known, the monastery library must have contained well over a hundred books, not counting duplicates – a truly prodigious library for the period, especially when we bear in mind that there must have been some additional books in it that Bede didn't use.

One surviving book that Bede almost certainly knew is the Codex[16] Laudianus, which is now in the Bodleian Library at Oxford. This is a text of the New Testament Book of Acts, written in parallel columns of Latin and Greek. The volume is thought to have originated in Sardinia, and to have arrived in England some time around the middle of the seventh century. It is called the Laudianus because it was once owned by William Laud, a controversial archbishop of Canterbury in the seventeenth century.

As well as acquiring, storing and reading books, the monks of Bede's monastery also created them in their own *scriptorium* or writing-room. They not only made fresh copies of books they had acquired or borrowed – they also made translations, compiled condensed versions of existing books (including books of extracts) and wrote commentaries on works of special value, such as the books of the Bible. The bulk of Bede's surviving writings are commentaries on Scripture, and he tells us that he also produced a condensed version of Adamnan's *On the holy places*, a sort of guide book to the Holy Land.

Bede's works on the Bible demonstrate a very good knowledge of Latin, but a less-than-complete knowledge of Greek and Hebrew. In fact Jenkins[17] insists that Bede may have had very little knowledge of Hebrew at all. In his biblical works, Bede sticks close to respected authorities from the past, so much so that Jenkins suggests that anyone who did a thorough survey of Bede on the Bible would be hard-pressed to identify which ideas were really new-sprung from the head of the Northumbrian.

Bede's interest in time, chronology and numbers in general show

---

16 The Latin word for a modern-style book with pages, as opposed to a scroll.
17 In Thompson (ed.): *Bede: His life, times and writings*, p. 152 ff.

themselves in his biblical works. In writing about the New Testament Book of Revelation, for instance, he tried to determine the meanings of the many baffling numbers that appear in that book. He also tried to make sense of the chronology of the Old Testament which, as we have seen, helped him to determine that the world was less than five thousand years old in what we call the eighth century.

In tackling the Old Testament, Bede, his contemporaries and the authorities he used were often on the prowl for signs that events in New Testament times and later were predicted in the Old Testament.

We have already seen how Bede saw the craftsmen of the temple of Solomon as representing the great scholars of the Christian Church. He also saw the white marble of the temple as a symbol of purity. The mountain on which the temple was built was a symbol of Christ – it was to this mountain that Abraham took Isaac to be sacrificed, and this sacrifice foreshadowed that of Jesus. The fact that there was once a threshing-floor on the mountain is a reminder that John the Baptist said Jesus would 'winnow his threshing floor' (Matthew 3:12).

Including his scientific, historical and biblical works, Bede is thought to have written at least thirty books. These would have swelled the library of his monastery very considerably, and through the process of lending and copying, Bede's books found their way into the libraries of other monasteries and churches. The surviving catalogues of these old libraries tell us that, for instance, St Augustine's at Canterbury had twenty works by Bede, while Bury St Edmunds had forty (perhaps a full set with the addition of some works attributed to the Northumbrian, but not actually written by him at all). Several libraries, including that at Durham, have what may be Bede autographs - books written out or copied by Bede with his own hand. Around the world, there are some 150 medieval manuscripts of Bede's *Ecclesiastical history* still in existence.

The most astounding extant product of the *scriptorium* (or *scriptoria*) of Wearmouth/Jarrow in Bede's time was not written by Bede, although it is hard to believe that the scholar had nothing to do with its production. This is the Codex Amiatinus, which is now in the Mediceo-Laurentian Library at Florence. The codex, which was identified as a product of Biscop's monastery during the nineteenth century, sits in this exquisite Italian city alongside many precious books of Dante, and a famous manuscript of Virgil from the fourth or fifth century, in a building designed by no less an architect than Michelangelo.

The Codex Amiatinus was an attempt to include the whole of the Bible, in the Latin version of St Jerome, in a single book. Since the parchment of the pages is heavy, and the writing comparatively large, the Codex Amiatinus is nearly eight inches thick, its eleven hundred pages each measuring roughly twenty by fourteen inches.

This gigantic book, which is taken around on a trolley at the Laurentian, is one of three made at Bede's monastery during the time of Abbot Ceolfrith. The churches of the twin monasteries got one each, and Ceolfrith planned to take what became the Codex Amiatinus to Rome as a gift for the pope. Unfortunately, the abbot died before he made it to the Eternal City with his lavish present.

The Amiatinus is not as elaborately decorated as the Lindisfarne Gospels or the Book of Kells. Its text pages are relatively plain, but there are picture-pages with deep, rich colours painted in a style reminiscent of Continental books of the same period. One of these pictures shows the Old Testament prophet Ezra writing in a book, much as Bede and his monkish brothers must have done.

Ezra sits on a stool before a tall book-case, writing in a volume that is propped up on his lap. His feet are on a wooden foot-stool, and various instruments lie on the ground in front of him, including a pair of dividers intended to be used, perhaps, for accurately spacing lines scored on the pages to be written on. The book-case behind Ezra is particularly interesting as, despite its size, it only contains nine books arranged on five shelves. The books are laid flat with their spines outwards for easy identification. The case has wooden doors so that it can be closed to protect the books inside from rodents, insects, smoke, fire and perhaps theft. The artist who created this picture of Ezra obviously imagined the prophet to be something like a scholarly bishop of Anglo-Saxon Northumbria, who used the technology the artist himself saw around him every day.

The picture is wildly anachronistic in that Ezra would have written on scrolls and would never have seen a codex. Ezra's book-case is decorated with some decidedly Christian symbols, and it is tempting to suggest that it is an affectionate portrait by one of the monk-illustrators of his favourite book-case in the monastery library. Such book-cases were the descendants of the niches in stone walls where scrolls and codices used to be kept, and the arks in synagogues where the Torah scrolls are stored.

It was thought that the two other Bibles Ceolfrith commissioned were completely lost, but in 1886 a Canon Greenwell of Durham found a page from one of the missing Bibles bound into a book of accounts on a book-stall in Newcastle. More leaves were discovered in Nottinghamshire in 1911, and in Dorset in 1982.

The production of such prestigious books as the Amiatinus and its sister volumes would have been a truly collaborative effort, involving contributions from all corners of the monastery community. The librarians (if they had any) would have been involved in ensuring that copy-texts were available, and others would have been in charge of the manufacture and supply of ink, paint, brushes, pens and parchment.

The preparation of parchment was itself a long process with many stages, and special workshops would probably have had to be constructed or commandeered for the accommodation of the various crafts involved. Making parchment would also have meant a great deal of handling of dead livestock, and if anthrax was one of the plagues that swept through the monastic houses, then working with diseased mammals, whether dead or alive, could have been a source of infection.

The style of the Codex Amiatinus is surprisingly Continental in flavour, and it is partly for this reason that the book was not recognised as a Northumbrian product for many centuries. The monks of Bede's *scriptorium* were either influenced by Continental models they had seen in their library, or were themselves foreign craftsmen imported from France or elsewhere.

V. THE ECCLESIASTICAL HISTORY

In writing his *Ecclesiatical history*, Bede turned to the monastery library for help, particularly with his accounts of events that happened centuries before his birth. The first date in Bede's history is 60BC, when Julius Caesar invaded Britain. Before that the historian gives a quick account of the arrival of the Britons, the Picts and the Scots (from Ireland), but Bede has no dates for these immigrations.

For events nearer to his own time, Bede combined what he found in books with his own original research. In his dedication of the *Ecclesiastical history* to Ceolwulf, Bede explains that, when it came to events outside Ceolwulf's kingdom of Northumbria, he relied on letters from known authorities, and even benefited from the researches of one Nothelm in the archives of Rome itself.

The Latin title of Bede's *Ecclesiastical history* is the *Historia ecclesiastica gentis Anglorum:* the use of the word *Anglorum* is a reminder that Bede's point of view is that of his own people, the Angles or Anglo-Saxons. These Germanic ancestors of Bede came to Britain in the early fifth century, and gradually forced the tribes of native British people westwards.

When they first came to Britain, the Anglo-Saxons were Pagans, although many of the British groups they warred against had been Christian since Roman times. Much of Bede's *Ecclesiastical history* is concerned with the process, which was slow and endured many setbacks, of converting the Anglo-Saxons (the original 'English') to Christianity.

One story in the *History* is supposed to describe the precise moment when the kingdom of Northumbria abandoned Paganism and took up the cross. King Edwin of Northumbria was visited by a missionary called Paulinus, who had been sent to Britain in 601, in the second wave of missionaries from Rome.

Unsure as to whether to become Christian, Edwin called a council of his thanes, who, after some discussion, came out in favour of the religion Paulinus had brought to them. One thane, who is unnamed but was obviously a man of a very poetic turn of mind, said that he thought life was like the swift passage of a sparrow through the hall of a great lord at night: he thought the surrounding night of death was something that Christianity could perhaps illuminate.

Convinced, the thanes agreed to be baptised with their king, and Coifi, a Pagan high-priest, defiled his old temple by throwing a spear at it and encouraging the thanes to burn it down. Previously, Coifi had complained to the king that although he had devoted his life to the old gods, they had shown him little kindness. All this happened in 627 at Goodmanham, to the east of York.

The story of Edwin's conference and the sudden conversion of Coifi is unusual for Bede in that it does not contain any supernatural elements, though a touch of magic comes from the profound image of the sparrow flying through the great hall on a winter's night. One example of a supernatural story is that of Caedmon, who is now recognised as the first known English poet. Caedmon worked at the monastery of Abbess Hilda at Streanaeshalch or, as we would now call it, Whitby. One night he was in a company of people there, who were taking turns to sing and play on the harp.

Caedmon thought that he couldn't sing, so when he saw the harp approaching him, he sneaked away and went to the stable, where it was his turn to sleep that night, to look out for the animals. A mysterious man appeared to him there in a dream, and told him to sing a song of all Creation. When he woke, Caedmon found he had the gift of inventing verses spontaneously, but only on religious themes. His God-given gift was recognised as such, and he was allowed to become a monk.

The English were converted to Christianity from two different directions – from the north-west by the Scots (originally an Irish group) and from the south-east by missionaries such as Augustine and Paulinus, sent from Rome. The Christianity that spread from the south-east was, broadly speaking, Roman Catholic, while the Christians who had been converted by Irish missionaries were of the distinctive 'Celtic Christian' type. Much of Bede's *History* is taken up with attempts by various people to bring the Celtic Christians around to the Roman Catholic way of doing things.

Bede lovingly re-tells tales of saints and martyrs from the different Christian groups in Britain, but he is very open about asserting that the Roman way was the right way, and that, virtuous as they may have been in some ways, Christians who were out of touch with the Roman way were in grave danger of missing the point of Christianity altogether.

The method used to calculate the date of Easter was seen as a crucial difference between the Celtic and Roman churches: Bede also identifies other features that a monastery in particular should have, to make it truly Roman. Time and again in his *History*, he describes how the correct celebration of Easter, the correct method of singing in church, and some means of communication with Rome itself tend to make a Christian community a Catholic community.

A pivotal event in Bede's *History* is the Synod of Whitby, which happened in the plague year of 664. At this synod, held in the presence of the Northumbrian king Oswiu, it was decided that the Christians of Northumbria should follow the Roman way, and abandon the Celtic practices.

In his *History*, Bede revisits some subjects he had already handled in previous writings. He writes extensively about the monk and bishop Cuthbert, although he had already written both a verse and prose life of this loveable saint, and must have known that there was already a perfectly good biography of the saint, written by an anonymous monk of Lindisfarne. Since Bede was about fifteen when Cuthbert died, he would have been able to speak to monks and others who had actually known him.

Bede also uses the pages of his *History* to revisit some of the events covered in his *Lives of the abbots of Wearmouth and Jarrow*.

VI. IN SEARCH OF BEDE

Although Bede was clearly grateful to be living in a time of peace, during the reign of the saintly King Ceolwulf, to whom he dedicated his *History*, he was no Polyanna about the state of Christianity among the English. In the surprisingly outspoken *Letter to Egbert*, which is probably his last surviving written work, he complains about lazy bishops who fail to visit the people who pay for their upkeep, and about churchmen who live lives devoted to eating, drinking and fornication.

Something for which Bede reserves particular scorn is the prevalence of what he clearly regards as 'fake' monasteries, where the inmates enjoy all the privileges of the monastic life but do not live under an authentic monastic Rule, such as that of St Benedict. Such monasteries, Bede asserts, take up land that could be used to yield income to finance more bishops, or to reward deserving followers of the king. Bede also felt that the monks in these places would be better employed as soldiers, fighting for their monarch.

It may be that the bitterness evident in the *Letter to Egbert* reflects Bede's awareness of his own failing health. The process of Bede's death is described in a moving letter written by his student Cuthbert. The letter, addressed to somebody called Cuthwin, is so detailed that it has the effect of bringing Bede's life into sharp focus just as he is about to come to the end of it.

If people are to be judged by the manner of their death, then Bede, on the evidence of the *Letter of Cuthbert*, was indeed a hard-working saint with a dedication to worship and to his scholarly pursuits. As we know, he was praying and singing psalms right up to the end.

We learn from Simeon of Durham and in the *Letter from Cuthbert* that Bede had his own cell – in this case probably a separate hut – on the monastery lands. This may have been a privilege granted to him in recognition of the importance of his literary work. Cuthbert's *Letter* and some details from Bede's introduction to the *Ecclesiastical history* suggest that Bede may have had a coterie of willing helpers who assisted him in his literary projects.

Almost with his last breath, Bede was dictating a translation into English of the *Gospel of John*, which suggests that the necessity of physically writing down what came into his head may have been removed from the scholar when it became too burdensome. Bede's helpers may also have read to him from his sources, and we know from the example of Nothelm, Bede's researcher in Rome, that fellow-monks could act as research assistants. Bede may also have had a sort of monkish secretary to deal with his correspondence.

This sort of arrangement, whereby the donkey-work of writing is done by someone else, is something that modern writers dream about, but only a few highly-paid authors can afford to have in place. The comparative isolation of Bede's cell is reminiscent of attempts by modern writers to work in attics, sheds, cabins or sections of houses isolated from the main body of the building. After his death, Bede's remains were probably placed in greater and even more privileged isolation, in a tomb in the church at Jarrow.

Illness and death seem not to have had the same terror for the more serious-minded monks of Bede's time as they hold for us today. Whereas we strive to avoid illness, and eagerly seek treatment as soon as it appears, it is clear from many of the biographies in Bede's *Ecclesiastical history* that holy men and women of his time greeted illness as a welcome trial of their own strength of faith, and viewed death as an escape from a flawed world and an opportunity to enter into eternal glory. Nevertheless, Bede cried as he approached death, and repeated a solemn phrase from the New Testament: 'It is a fearful thing to fall into the hands of the living God' (Hebrews 10:31).

No doubt the Northumbrian scholar hoped that the monastery to which he had contributed so much would grow and thrive throughout future centuries, its security guarded by the actions of strong and pious kings. As a historian, Bede may have suspected that this might not happen, though he could not have predicted the precise nature of the decline of Wearmouth/Jarrow as a religious and cultural centre.

The locations of the twin monasteries near the mouths of rivers made them easier to get to, and to travel from, since substantial sections of long-distance journeys in Bede's time were often done by water. We have seen how the the placing of the monasteries may have made them particularly liable to bubonic plague – in the last years of the ninth century they fell victim to another plague – Viking raids.

The Vikings left the monasteries devastated, and there may have been little or no occupation of the sites by monks until the eleventh century, when the community was revived.

Although the precious books and church plate the Vikings didn't get hold of were probably moved to safety by the monks, one treasure remained at Jarrow – the bones of Bede.

The presence of a famous set of bones could be a great asset to a church or monastery, as it tended to raise the general prestige of the place, and could attract pilgrims, and donations from the pious. It may be for this reason that, in the early part of the eleventh century, the precious remains of Bede were removed from their resting-place at Jarrow.

The agent of this move – or the bone-thief as we may call him, was Ælfred, a presbyter of Durham. Ælfred was responsible for extracting the bones of many Northumbrian saints and martyrs from their ancient resting-places and depositing them at Durham – these included St Cuthbert's old master Boisil of Melrose, two bishops, two abbesses and a king – Oswin.

Ælfred was in the habit of praying all night at Bede's grave in Jarrow on the anniversary of the scholar's death. It seems that one night, he stole Bede's bones and made off with them alone. The eleventh century historian Simeon of Durham tells us that the bones of Bede spent some time 'in a little linen bag' inside the tomb of one of his heroes, St Cuthbert. This tomb was by then shared by such remains as the head of St Oswald.

Bede would no doubt have felt honoured to be lying in the company of so many saints that he had read of and written about, but he must have had feelings of attachment to Wearmouth and Jarrow that he could not have felt for Durham, which was an unimportant little place in his day.

Durham Cathedral was preceded by a succession of churches on the same site, the first of them being a simple shelter for the miraculously preserved body of Cuthbert, which arrived there in 995. The story goes that the Viking threat forced the monks of Lindisfarne to flee with Cuthbert's body, and that after many travels and a long stay at Chester-le-Street, the saint became the most precious relic of what was to become Durham Cathedral.

Bede would have been astonished at the size and sumptuousness of the last church to be raised around Cuthbert's bones – the cathedral that still stands over them today. He would also have been puzzled by the alien look of the place, built in the Norman style which he would never have seen in eighth-century Britain.

In 1370, when Dante had been dead for nearly fifty years and Bede for over six hundred, the latter's bones were moved to the Galilee chapel at the west end of the cathedral, where they still lie today. Until the Reformation, the relics lay in a 'fereter' or shrine of gold and silver, which could be picked up and carried by monks in procession on certain holy days. Now Bede lies in a grave under the flag-stones of the chapel.

It seems that Bede was never as popular as St Cuthbert, who lies at the opposite end of Durham Cathedral. In medieval times, Durham attracted thousands of pilgrims because of the presence there of Bede's older contemporary, but we might say that whereas people came *into* the cathedral to see Cuthbert, the lines of Bede's reputation and influence radiated *outwards* to wherever history and scholarship were and are respected. And Cuthbert never made it into Dante's *Divine Comedy*.

Readers in search of Bede beyond the pages of books could do worse than to visit his tomb in Durham, and the remains of the monastery churches at Wearmouth and Jarrow. In the tradition of English church architecture, these buildings have been extensively remodelled, but there is still much to see that will evoke monastic life in the eighth century.

At Jarrow, walls that Bede would have known as part of the monastery church are still part of St Paul's, though in his time the interior would probably have glowed with gorgeous icons fetched from the Continent by Benedict Biscop and others.

Also at Jarrow, there is now a museum called Bede's World, where Saxon-period buildings have been recreated, and live farm-animals of the type Bede would have known stand around in Saxon-style paddocks.

Threatened by plague and invasion in earlier centuries, Wearmouth and Jarrow found themselves in the middle of a boom in heavy industry in more recent times. It seems that for many years the captains of cargo vessels would dump their ballast in the very graveyard of St Peter's, Wearmouth, so that the Saxon porch there had to be dug out in 1855.

Early in the twenty-first century, it is in some ways easier to picture Bede's time than it must have been in the early twentieth. If Dante had travelled through time and space to see Jarrow and Wearmouth in the early years of the twentieth century, he might have been reminded of his own *Inferno*. This scene of 'dark satanic mills' was described rather well in a 1907 lecture[18] on Bede given by Canon Rawnsley in Sunderland town hall:

And what a book of the revelation of God in nature had he [Bede] not to read in, when in this country instead of dreary cinder-heaps, and pit-chimneys plumed with smoke all day, and coke-ovens with fearful eyes, and blast-furnaces spouting flame all night, and rivers running black and turbid to the sea, he had, wherever he turned, wooded dell and sunny moor and glittering stream and glimmering sea to be his daily counsellors for God!

VII. THE JUDGEMENT OF HISTORY

It is hard to overestimate the achievement or the importance of Bede. As Dante's interest in him shows, he was considered to be a figure of great influence well into the Middle Ages. His *Ecclesiastical history* was first translated into English, or what we would call Old English, in the ninth century, and this translation may have been commissioned

---

18 *The Venerable Bede: His life and work*, Hills & Co, 1907

by the great King Alfred himself. There are currently at least three modern English translations of this remarkable book in print. Bede's biography of Cuthbert, and his history of his own monastery, are also in print in the modern English that developed from the Old English of the Anglo-Saxons.

Historians wanting to cover a whole swathe of English and Continental history around the time of Bede have no choice but to consult his historical writings, and Bede's characteristic approach to writing history gives many clues as to the mind-set of his age.

Bede's credulous approach to miracles, which swarm all over the pages of his *Ecclesiastical history*, has confused some modern historians who, it would seem, would like Bede to be a more rational and less pious historian. For Bede to have done this would have been for him to abandon the Great Cause of English Christians in his time, which was to widen and deepen the Christianity that had only recently taken hold among the Anglo-Saxon people.

Considering such works as Bede's histories, and artefacts like the stupendous Codex Amiatinus, it seems incredible that achievements of such world-wide importance could have been accomplished in out-of-the-way places like Wearmouth and Jarrow. This is a reminder that 'golden ages' of great influence and creativity can spring up anywhere where the right conditions prevail. In Bede's case, these conditions seem to have included the right mix of isolation and connection with the outside world, the enthusiastic contributions of a whole community, and a few years of precious peace.

APPENDIX:
FROM LONGFELLOW'S TRANSLATION OF
DANTE'S *PARADISO*, CANTO X

Lights many saw I, vivid and triumphant,
Make us a centre and themselves a circle,
More sweet in voice than luminous in aspect.

Thus girt about the daughter of Latona
We sometimes see, when pregnant is the air,
So that it holds the thread which makes her zone.

Within the court of Heaven, whence I return,
Are many jewels found, so fair and precious
They cannot be transported from the realm;

And of them was the singing of those lights.
Who takes not wings that he may fly up thither,
The tidings thence may from the dumb await!

As soon as singing thus those burning suns
Had round about us whirled themselves three times,
Like unto stars neighbouring the steadfast poles,

Ladies they seemed, not from the dance released,
But who stop short, in silence listening
Till they have gathered the new melody.

And within one I heard beginning: "When
The radiance of grace, by which is kindled
True love, and which thereafter grows by loving,

Within thee multiplied is so resplendent
That it conducts thee upward by that stair,
Where without reascending none descends,

Who should deny the wine out of his vial
Unto thy thirst, in liberty were not
Except as water which descends not seaward.

Fain wouldst thou know with what plants is enflowered
This garland that encircles with delight
The Lady fair who makes thee strong for Heaven.

Of the lambs was I of the holy flock
Which Dominic conducteth by a road
Where well one fattens if he strayeth not.

He who is nearest to me on the right
My brother and master was; and he Albertus[19]
Is of Cologne, I Thomas of Aquinum[20].

If thou of all the others wouldst be certain,
Follow behind my speaking with thy sight
Upward along the blessed garland turning.

That next effulgence issues from the smile
Of Gratian[21], who assisted both the courts
In such wise that it pleased in Paradise.

The other which near by adorns our choir
That Peter[22] was who, e'en as the poor widow,
Offered his treasure unto Holy Church.

The fifth light, that among us is the fairest,
Breathes forth from such a love, that all the world
Below is greedy to learn tidings of it.

Within it is the lofty mind, where knowledge
So deep was put, that, if the true be true,
To see so much there never rose a second[23].

Thou seest next the lustre of that taper,
Which in the flesh below looked most within
The angelic nature and its ministry[24].

Within that other little light is smiling
The advocate of the Christian centuries,
Out of whose rhetoric Augustine was furnished[25].

Now if thou trainest thy mind's eye along

---

19 Albertus Magnus
20 Thomas Aquinas
21 Franciscus Gratianus
22 Peter the Lombard
23 Solomon
24 Dionysius the Areopagite
25 Paulus Orosius

From light to light pursuant of my praise,
With thirst already of the eighth thou waitest.

By seeing every good therein exults
The sainted soul, which the fallacious world
Makes manifest to him who listeneth well;

The body whence 'twas hunted forth is lying
Down in Cieldauro, and from martyrdom
And banishment it came unto this peace[26].

See farther onward flame the burning breath
Of Isidore[27], of Beda[28], and of Richard[29]
Who was in contemplation more than man.

This, whence to me returneth thy regard,
The light is of a spirit unto whom
In his grave meditations death seemed slow.

It is the light eternal of Sigier[30],
Who, reading lectures in the Street of Straw,
Did syllogize invidious verities."

Then, as a horologe that calleth us
What time the Bride of God is rising up
With matins to her Spouse that he may love her,

Wherein one part the other draws and urges,
Ting! ting! resounding with so sweet a note,
That swells with love the spirit well disposed,

Thus I beheld the glorious wheel move round,
And render voice to voice, in modulation
And sweetness that can not be comprehended,

Excepting there where joy is made eternal.

---

26 Boethius
27 Isidore of Seville
28 Bede
29 Richard of St Victor
30 Sigier of Brabant

BIBLIOGRAPHY

Alighieri, Dante: *The divine comedy III: Paradise* (trans. Sayers, D.L. & Reynolds, B.), Penguin, 2004

Alighieri, Dante: *The divine comedy: Hell, Purgatory, Paradise* (trans. Longfellow, H.W.), Chartwell, 2006

Backhouse, Janet: *The scriptorium of Wearmouth/Jarrow*, The Bede Monastery Museum, 1985

Bede: *The ecclesiastical history of the English people* (trans. McClure, Judith & Collins, Roger), Oxford, 1999

Bede: *A history of the English church and people* (trans. Sherley-Price, Leo), Penguin, 1968

Bede: *The reckoning of time* (trans. Wallis, Faith), Liverpool UP, 1999

St Benedict: *The Rule of St Benedict* (trans. Abbot Parry), Gracewing, 1990

Billings, R.W.: *Architectural antiquities of the county of Durham*, Boone, 1843

Billings, R.W.: *Architectural illustrations and description of the cathedral church at Durham*, Boone, 1843

Bonner, G.W. (ed.): *Famulus Christi: Essays in commemoration of the thirteenth centenary of the birth of the Venerable Bede*, SPCK, 1976

Colgrave, Bertram (trans. & ed.): *Two lives of St Cuthbert*, Cambridge, 1985

Defoe, Daniel: *A journal of the plague year*, Penguin, 1966

Garbutt, George: *A historical and descriptive view of the parishes of Monkwearmouth and Bishopwearmouth, and the port and borough of Sunderland*, Garbutt, 1819

Glasswell, Samantha: *The earliest English: Living and dying in Anglo-Saxon England*, Tempus, 2002

Heaney, Seamus: *Beowulf: a verse translation*, Norton, 2002

Hegge, Robert: *The legend of St Cuthbert*, Simon Webb, 2009

Hyslop, Robert: *St Peter's Church, Monkwearmouth*, B.P.C., [after 1946]

Pevsner, Nikolaus (rev. Williamson, Elizabeth): *The buildings of England: County Durham*, Penguin, 1985

Raine, James: *St Cuthbert*, Andrews, 1828

Canon Rawnsley: *The Venerable Bede: His life and work*, Hills & Co, 1907

Rose, J.D.: *Jarrow church and monastery*, J.D. Rose, 1932

Rosen, William: *Justinian's flea*, Jonathan Cape, 2006

Simeon of Durham: *A history of the church of Durham*, Llanerch, 1993

Stranks, C.J.: *The Venerable Bede*, SPCK, 1955

Surtees Society: *The Rites of Durham*, Andrews, 1902

Thompson, A.H.: *Bede: His life, times and writings*, Oxford, 1935

Toynbee, Paget (ed.): *The letters of Dante*, Oxford, 1920

Virgil: *The Aeneid* (trans. Dryden, John), Airmont, 1968

Webb, J.F. (trans.): *The age of Bede*, Penguin, 1998

Webb, Simon: *Nicholas Breakspear: The pope from England*, The Langley Press, 2009

Wormald, Patrick: *The times of Bede*, Blackwell, 2006

Also by Simon Webb:

In search of the Northern Saints
ISBN 978-0954475970

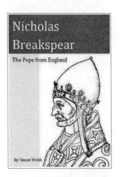

Nicholas Breakspear: The pope from England
ISBN 978-0-9564551-0-9

For details of more of Simon's books,
please visit his websites at:
http://sites.google.com/site/simonsbooks/
https://sites.google.com/site/thelangleypress/